THE POCKET

Scouse English

Published in 2024
by Gemini Adult Books Ltd
Part of Gemini Books Group

Based in Woodbridge and London
Marine House, Tide Mill Way
Woodbridge, Suffolk IP12 1AP
United Kingdom

www.geminibooks.com

Part of the Gemini Pocket series

Cover image: Sabena Jane Blackbird/Alamy Stock Photo

ISBN 978-1-83616-004-5

A CIP catalogue record for this book is available from the British Library.

Printed in China

10 9 8 7 6 5 4 3 2 1

FSC www.fsc.org
MIX
Paper | Supporting responsible forestry
FSC® C008047

THE POCKET

Scouse English

G:

Contents

Introduction

From 'trabs' for trainers to 'Z-Cars' for the police, understand both the roots and key words of one of England's most widely recognized dialects.

Before the Second World War, Scouse was not much heard outside Liverpool, but when The Beatles stormed the charts, the whole world became familiar with the dialect.

'Lob-scouse', or simply scouse, was a stew brought to the port of Liverpool by sailors from Scandinavia. Made from cheap cuts of meat, it was once the staple diet of Liverpool's working class. Its popularity led to Liverpudlians being dubbed Scousers, and their dialect Scouse.

The nineteenth century saw a large influx of people into Liverpool from all parts of England, Scotland, Wales and

especially Ireland, bringing with them a rich mixture of regional accents, giving birth to the unique Scouse dialect.

During the 1940s, Scouse was brought to the UK's ears through radio by comedians such as Tommy Handley. Television has continued to showcase Scouse comedians, notably Ken Dodd, also, sitcoms such as *The Liver Birds* and later, *Brookside* and *Bread.* Alan Bleasdale, Carla Lane, Jimmy McGovern and Willy Russell dug deep into the Liverpool psyche to produce TV dramas and films about what it was like to live in 1980s' Merseyside, like Bleasdale's *Boys from the Blackstuff.*

Liverpool's iconic Superlambanana sculpture, which appears throughout the book, is 5.2 metres tall and weighs 8 tons. It was conceived by New York-based artist Taro Chiezo, who intended it in part as a comment on the dangers of genetic engineering. It also reflects common cargoes in the history of Liverpool's docks.

SCOUSE
-
ENGLISH

A

A

SCOUSE	ENGLISH
aah-eh	not fair!
ace!	well done!; also a noun, e.g., *'all right ace'*
ackers	cash
ahr	our, e.g., *'ahr kid'*
ale 'ouse	pub
ali	barber (Ali Baba), hairdresser
allus	always
amany	several
antwakky	antique, old-fashioned
are-eh	a complaint of misfortune or unfairness, e.g., *'Are-eh, that's proper arlas that.'*
arl	mean or unfair person or act (see also **arlas**)
arlas	very unfair, rude (see also **arl**), e.g., *'That exam was arlas. Bet I failed.'*

SCOUSE	ENGLISH
arl fella	dad ('old fellow')
auld	old
axe	ask, e.g., *'Dunno, don't axe me!'*

arrers

darts

In the 1930s, darts were banned in some parts of the UK, including Liverpool, where it was believed they encouraged drunkenness. Such bans were lifted only after the Second World War.

B

B

bevvie

alcoholic drink

Bevvie, derived from 'beverage' for an alcoholic drink, appears to have been in use since the early years of the twentieth century, with 'bevvy' as a verb recorded in the USA in 1908. Being 'bevvied' or 'bevvied up' for 'drunk and a 'bevvy-up', or drinking session, have also been recorded since the 1960s.

SCOUSE	ENGLISH
bag'ead	heroin addict
bags	lots
bail	run away
Baltic	very cold
bang	harm someone, e.g., *'I'll bang you, lad.'*
barney	argument
beak	cocaine, also a judge
beast, beastie	great, boss
bellend	idiot
bells	o'clock, e.g., *'See you at seven bells.'*
bender	(i) prolonged drinking session
	(ii) suspended jail sentence
bevvied	drunk

B

SCOUSE	ENGLISH
bezzy	best
biddie	woman (usually an old woman)
biff	poor person, idiot
bifta	cigarette
big girl's blouse	a male wimp
bill	alone, on one's own, e.g., *'I'm on my bill.'*
billy	a loner
binnie	binman
bins	sunglasses, spectacles, glasses
bizzie	the police
blag	talk your way out of something or convince someone of something, e.g., *'He blagged himself into that job.'*
blert	idiot
blind scouse	meatless stew

SCOUSE	ENGLISH
blitzed	drunk
blow	take a break from work
bluey	five-pound note (see **flim**)
bobbin	unauthorized time off work
boff	fart
Bootle buck	hard-faced biddie (woman)
boozer	pub
boss	excellent
boxed	pregnant
boxer	coffin-maker
brassic	penniless
buggeroo	naughty boy
busy, busies	policeman, policemen
bute	a know-it-all, a snob
butty	sandwich

C

C

casey

old-fashioned leather football

An old-style lace-up football made from many leather panels, which would increase dramatically in weight when wet. A kid with a 'caseyball' was popular as it was possible to have a proper game rather than struggling with a 'flyaway'.

SCOUSE	ENGLISH
cackhanded	inept, left-handed
cadge	beg, borrow
can't half	really good, e.g., *'He can't half play footy* (football).'
cat	goalkeeper, e.g., a *'top cat'* is a good goalkeeper
catlick	(i) Roman Catholic
	(ii) a light wash
chemicked	drunk
chest	a well-muscled person, e.g., *'He's a chest, him.'*
chief	thief
chiefed	stolen
chippy	fish and chip shop
chokka	full

C

SCOUSE	ENGLISH
chоss	chaos
chuck	(i) food
	(ii) throw; and, occasionally, the equivalent of the nearby Lancashire term of endearment, *'luv'*
chuffed	happy
class	really good
clever	healthy, e.g., *'I'm not feelin' too clever.'*

ciggie

cigarette

Ciggie, like 'bevvie', appears to have crossed the Atlantic from the USA at some point following 1908, but it's also a fairly typical Scouse contraction.

SCOUSE	ENGLISH
clobber	clothes
cob on	sulking, angry, e.g., *'He has a cob on.'*
college pud	student
come 'ed	come on ('come ahead')
cop shop	police station
corpy	Liverpool City Council
cozzie	swimming costume
crack	good time
cracker!	great!
crack on	recognize
creased	tired
Crimbo	Christmas

D

D

SCOUSE	ENGLISH
dairty	filthy
dale	they will, e.g., *'Dale do dat.'*
damage	cost, price
darrel	that will, e.g., *'Darrel do.'*
dat	that
dead	really, very, e.g., *'dead 'andy'* is very convenient, *'dead 'andsome'* is very good-looking and *'dead smart'* is very clever
dead ringer/dead spit	exactly alike
dekko	a look, to look
dem	those
devoed, devo'd	devastated, e.g., *'He was devo'd that he'd missed his train.'*
dick	detective (now obsolete)

diddy

little

The Diddymen, along with the Treacle and Jam Butty Mines of Knotty Ash, were the invention of Liverpool comedian Arthur Askey. Ken Dodd helped to make famous this supposed miniature race of people who inhabited his and Askey's home town of Knotty Ash.

D

SCOUSE	ENGLISH
dig out	clean, e.g., *'Gotta dig out me gaff.'*
dipper	pickpocket
dirty bastard	a Mancunian (person from Manchester)
divvy	stupid, a stupid person
do in	to beat someone up or damage or injure something, e.g., *'I'll do you in!'* or *'I did in my back.'*
do one	run away
doddle	(i) easy, e.g., *'It's a doddle.'*
	(ii) that will do, e.g., *'Doddle do okay.'*
dodgy	(i) risky
	(ii) suspect goods
doins	See **thingy**
doll	girl, woman (almost obsolete)
dolled up	overdressed

SCOUSE	ENGLISH
done up	overdressed
dozey	stupid
duff up	beat up
dur	there
dursent	dare not

duff

defective, pregnant

Duff, meaning something worthless or fake, like counterfeit money or smuggled goods, has been in use since as far back as 1781. In Liverpool, it's still going strong – 'I've just been 'ad off at the boozer with a duff telly.' Can also mean 'pregnant', as in 'up the duff'.

E · F

E · F

SCOUSE	ENGLISH
eee	expression of disgust or disapproval, e.g., *'Eee, look at that dozey get.'*
emmy oggie	empty house
eorta	he really should
ere!	excuse me!
feller	husband (originally, but now can be a male companion of any description)
fetch	bring
filth	police
firebobby	a fireman
fit	good-looking
footy	football

flim

five-pound note

Flim, a contraction of 'flimsy', for a banknote, appears to have been in use as far back as the nineteenth century. Its first recorded use for a fiver, a five-pound note, is in 1934.

G

G

gaff

home, house, residence

A gaff was originally (1819) any public place of amusement, such as a low-class theatre or music hall. It was only in the 1930s that it came to mean a house or shop. A Scouser's home is his or her gaff.

SCOUSE	ENGLISH
gaffer	boss, foreman
gaffless	homeless
gary	ecstasy tablet (after Gary Ablett)
gear	illegal drugs
gear!	marvellous!
geg	to interrupt or be nosy
get	idiot, sometimes preceded by dozey
ghost	accompanying a workmate and watching him work, but doing nothing oneself
gimme	give me, e.g., *'Gimme a ciggy.'*
gissa	give us, e.g., *'Gissa job!'* (see **gimme**, also **gizza**)
gizza	give us (as above)
gizzit	give it to me

G

SCOUSE	ENGLISH
gob	(i) mouth
	(ii) to spit
go 'ed	go on, or okay then ('go ahead')
goolies	testicles
goosed	exhausted
goosegog	gooseberry
gorra	got a, e.g., *'Gorra ciggy?'*
gorrany	do you have any, e.g., *'Gorrany ciggies?'*
gorrup	overdressed
gozzie	(i) cross-eyed
	(ii) contraceptives
graft	work
grass	inform, informer

SCOUSE	ENGLISH
gripped	to be caught doing something
grock	phlegm; also a large, intimidating person

grotty

squalid

Grotty, a shortened form of 'grotesque', was first used in the 1960s as a general term of disapproval, to mean unpleasant, squalid, ugly, etc. – as in, 'His gaff is dead grotty' or 'She's feeling really grotty'.

4·1

in bulk

laughing a lot

While an English dictionary definition of 'bulk' would be along the lines of 'great or considerable volume', in Scouse, 'in bulk' means laughing fit to burst – 'She was so funny she had me in bulk!'

SCOUSE	ENGLISH
head	someone who is physically tough; also used as a suffix, e.g., *'You mad'ead.'*
hold on!	wait a moment!
hooter	nose
iddle	it will, e.g., *'Iddle do dat.'*
in a bit	goodbye
is right	an expression of support, approval or agreement
it's all going off	a physical fight

J·K

J·K

SCOUSE	ENGLISH
jack	detective (now obsolete)
jar	glass of beer
jarg	broken, fake; also fake designer clothes
jerry	chamber pot
jew	do you, e.g., *'Jew wanna ciggie?'*
jib it	abandon a task
jigger	back entry or alley
jobe	taxi
jockey	driver
judy	girl, young woman (semi-obsolete)
judy scuffer	a policewoman
kaylied	drunk
ketwig	a 10–15-year-old boy with on-trend hair

SCOUSE	ENGLISH
kid brother	younger brother (though can sometimes mean 'older brother' and occasionally even a sister)
kidda	affectionate term for kid brother; also lad, mate
Kirkby kiss	headbutt
khazi	toilet
knackers	testicles

kecks

underpants, trousers

The Scouse use of 'kecks' to mean trousers, initially, then, more recently, underpants appears to date back to the early 1960s.

L

L

SCOUSE	ENGLISH
lamp	(i) strike hard
	(ii) surreptitiously watch
lanny	Mersey ferry landing stage
lar	lad, friend, e.g., *'All right, lar?'*
lar lar	Scouser with a pronounced accent
latchlifter	price of half a pint of ale
laughin'	good
lavvy	toilet
lecky	electricity, e.g., a *'lecky man'* is a meter reader and a *'lecky board'* is an electricity company

left-footer

Roman Catholic

Most spades used for digging in Britain and Ireland have a foot-rest at the top of their blade. Two-sided spades have a foot-rest on both sides of the shaft, but there is an older style which has just a single foot-rest. It's thought that two-sided spades were introduced into Ireland by Protestant 'planters' in the sixteenth century, where they became widely used throughout Ulster. One-sided spades continued to be used in the overwhelmingly Catholic south and west. In reality, the two-sided spade of Ulster was generally used with the left foot, while the one-sided spade tended to be used with the right foot. But the 'wrong foot', which Catholics were accused of using by Protestants, has come to be thought of as the left foot, hence 'left-footer'.

L

lolly ice

ice lolly

While most of the UK might say 'ice lolly', like Americans, if you were brought up in Liverpool, or most places in the north-west of England, it was a 'lolly ice'.

SCOUSE	ENGLISH
leg it	run away
lemme	let me, allow me
lennus	loan me
like	equivalent of 'you know', e.g., '*He can't half play footy, like!*'
loosie	a loose cigarette
lorra	large amount, e.g., '*Gorra lorra money.*'
lushed	hopelessly drunk
luzz	throw

M

M

SCOUSE	ENGLISH
made up	happy, pleased
mam	mother
mate	sir (this has now replaced the obsolete '**wack**', '**wacker**', '**tosh**' and '**mush**' as a greeting)
meff	idiot, e.g., *'I wouldn't share a room with him, he's a bit of a meff.'*
mennal	insane
merry	slightly drunk
messy	intoxicated
miladdo!	my old friend! (not always spoken in a friendly tone)
milkie	milkman
ming	an annoying person
mingy	mean, stingy
mitts	hands
mobie	mobile phone

SCOUSE	ENGLISH
moggy	cat
mouth!	you're talking too much!
mush	mate (now obsolete)

marmalize

beat up

'Marmalize' is said to have been popularized by Liverpool comedian Ken Dodd. Supposedly, it is a mash-up of 'marmalade' and 'pulverize'.

N

N

SCOUSE	ENGLISH
nan	grandmother (sometimes pronounced 'nin')
nob'ead	idiot
nick	versatile noun or verb, meaning:
	(i) arrest
	(ii) steal
	(iii) prison
	(iv) police station
nicker	pound
nix	nothing
nouse	intelligence
nut	See **Kirkby kiss**
nuts	testicles
nutt'n	nothing

Nitty Nora

school nurse

Nitty Nora, the bug explorer, or head explorer, would check schoolchildren's hair for nits, the eggs of head lice.

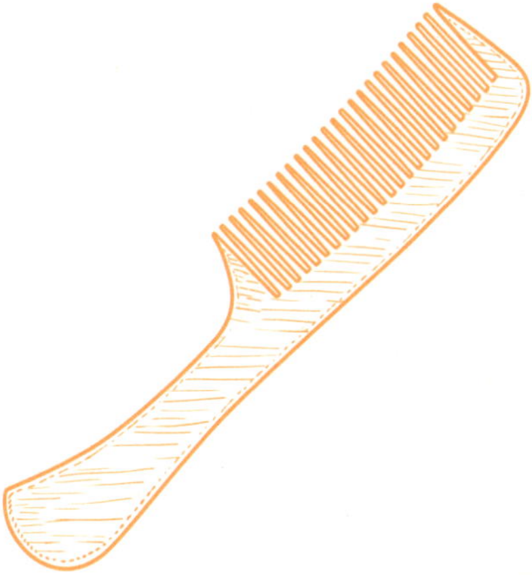

O·P

O·P

SCOUSE	ENGLISH
oavy	overtime
offie	off-licence, corner shop (selling alcohol)
on top!	out of order!
oodles	large amount
oojah	See **thingy**
our kid	a sibling or close relative
outer	out of, e.g., *'outer work'*
owl	older person, e.g., an '*owl feller'* is a father and an '*owl girl'* is a mother
ozzy	hospital
pairm	hairdo
palatick	helplessly drunk
penguin house	a convent
petty toilet	an outside toilet

SCOUSE	ENGLISH
plums	testicles
prezzie	present
privvy	toilet
Prod	a Protestant
Proddies	Protestants
properly	very, e.g. *'That's properly good'* (pronounced 'prop'ly')
pure	really, a lot, e.g., *'I was pure palatick.'*

Q·R

rozzer

policeman

Rozzer, a slang term for a police officer, has been in use since at least 1888. Some think that it is a shortening of the name of Sir Robert Peel, who founded the Metropolitan Police Service when he was UK home secretary in the 1820s (as are 'peeler' and 'bobby').

SCOUSE	ENGLISH
queen	term of endearment for a female
rem	idiot
rennie	rent collector
rob	steal
ropy	doubtful quality
rotten	very drunk
runs	diarrhoea

S

S

SCOUSE	ENGLISH
sanny	environmental health inspector
sarney	sandwich
scally	rogue (in the sense of a 'loveable rogue'); originally 'scallywag'
scarper	run away
scatty	dirty, disgusting
scoff	food
scone'ead	idiot
Scouser	inhabitant of Liverpool. See also **Scouse**
scran	food

Scouse

type of meat stew, dialect spoken in Liverpool

Scouse is Liverpool's traditional dish, a stew made with lamb, beef or a combination of both. The word is derived from 'lobscouse' (*lapskaus* in Scandinavia), a sailor's stew popular throughout northern Europe. Because of the popularity of this stew, Liverpudlians are known as Scousers, and their speech as Scouse.

S

scrat end

burnt chips

'Scrat' means a small portion or part of anything, derived from the verb form of the same word, which means to scratch in the ground for food. 'Scrat end' describes the overdone bits and pieces of chips left over in the fryer at a chippy, sold cheaply at the end of the evening.

SCOUSE	ENGLISH
screw	burgle
scuffer	policeman
shady	dubious, unfair
short-arse	small
show	mess, e.g., *'Her make-up looked an absolute show.'*
shop	See **grass**
shtum!	shut up!
sit off	do nothing
sketchy	dodgy
skinny	sly, unfair. See also **mingy**
skint	See **brassic**
slog	work, e.g., *'It's a hard slog 'ere, mate.'*
sloobag	promiscuous person

S

SCOUSE	ENGLISH
slummie	small change
sly	devious, nefarious, sordid, e.g., *'That's sly, that!'*
smart	great, brilliant; also, good health
smashing it	doing really well
sniff	inform on welfare cheats
snitch	steal
sock	robber from a disreputable district
soft lad	idiot (a term of endearment or aggression depending on context)
soft ollie	a stupid person
sound	good, well; also, I agree
sound!	excellent!
sowsh	social security
spaceman	stupid (also **space cadet**)

sound as a pound

great

The prominent sense of *sund* in Middle English was unhurt, uninjured or unwounded, echoing northern European languages – *gezond* in Dutch and *gesund* in German, meaning healthy. The first recorded use of 'sound as a pound' is in 'Anfield Rap' by C. Johnston in 1988.

S

SCOUSE	ENGLISH
spaced out	high on drugs
sparrer legs	thin legs ('sparrow legs')
spoon	to kick a ball badly, to make a mistake
stash	(i) hide
	(ii) hidden goods, usually stolen (formerly a sailor's belongings)
stoned	high on drugs
straight (up)	honest, e.g., *'Straight, I didn't do it!'*
straightener	fight
sup	drink
sussed	found out
sussies	suspenders (now a rare sight)
swede	head, e.g., *'She's doing my swede in.'*
swipe	steal

spends

money

Money to spend on oneself, often with respect to children's pocket money.

T

T

SCOUSE	ENGLISH
ta	thanks
tabs	drugs
talent	attractive male or female (sometimes applied collectively)
ta-ra	goodbye
tatty'ead	someone with a scruffy haircut
tear-arse	uncontrollable
thingy	any person, place or object which does not immediately spring to mind
tip	municipal rubbish dump
tizzie	over-excited
tod	alone
tosh	mate (now obsolete)

togga

football

Also spelled 'togger', a game of football, seemingly a peculiarly Scouse word, unfamiliar even to 'wools' and 'mancs' according to at least one Scouser now living in the south.

T

trabs

trainers

The origin of ‘trabs’ for trainers is thought to lie in the Adidas Trimm Trab trainer, popular in the 1980s. In the mid-1970s, there was a government-led sport and fitness campaign in Germany with the slogan, ‘Trimm Dich durch Sport’ (‘Get fit through sport’). Adidas launched the Trimm Trab ‘athleisure’ shoe. Discovered by travelling football fans, it made its way back to the UK, particularly Liverpool.

SCOUSE	ENGLISH
took	spoken for
tottie	girl, woman
trackies	tracksuit bottoms
trainies	trainers (see also **trabs** and **webs**)
twirlie	female pensioner
two dogs fight'n	Huyton (a district of Liverpool)

U·W

U·W

SCOUSE	ENGLISH
ullo	how are you?
us	me
wack	mate (now obsolete)
wanna	would like to
wayo!	just a moment!
webs	trainers (see also **trabs** and **trainies**)
well away	becoming drunk
west	peculiar, unusual
whacker	someone who doesn't come from Liverpool

wet nelly

cake, weakling

A wet nelly cake is a moister Liverpool version of Lancashire's Nelson fruit cake, hence its name. Also, a weakling.

woollyback

someone who isn't a Scouser

Woollyback is thought to derive from the practice of men using a sheep's fleece to protect their back when delivering coal from the mines surrounding Liverpool in the early years of the twentieth century.

SCOUSE	ENGLISH
whip	steal
whopper	someone prone to exaggeration
wild	diarrhoea
wool	a non-Liverpudlian living in an area close to Liverpool (see also **woollyback**)
worra	what a, e.g., *'Worra lorra money!'*
worral	what will, e.g., *'Worral 'appen?'*
wreck	to hurt or cause discomfort, e.g., *'That's wreckin' my 'ead.'*
wrecked	drunk

Y · Z

Y·Z

SCOUSE	ENGLISH
yer	you
yer wha'?	pardon?
yew	you (accusingly)
yews	you (plural)
yerrokay!	for God's sake, shut up!
zarrafact?	I don't believe you

Z-Cars

the police

Z-Cars was a 1960s BBC TV drama set in the fictional town of Newton, near Liverpool, based on Kirkby in the Liverpool borough of Knowsley. It ran for 801 episodes between 1962 and 1978. Brian Blessed played PC 'Fancy' Smith.

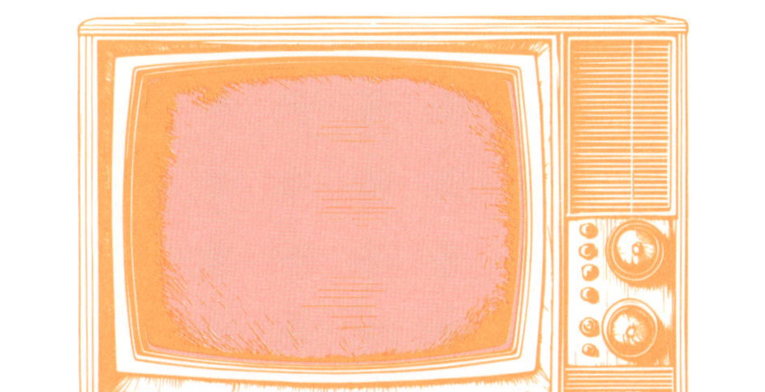

ENGLISH - SCOUSE

A

ENGLISH	SCOUSE
abandon a task	jib it
agreement	sound as a pound
alcoholic drink	bevvie
alone	tod, bill
always	allus
angry	cob on
annoying person	ming
antique	antwakky
approval or **agreement,** expression of	is right
argument	barney
arrest	nick
ask	axe
attractive male or female (also plural)	talent

B

ENGLISH	SCOUSE
back alley	jigger
barber	ali (Ali Baba)
beat up	do in, duff up, marmalize
becoming drunk	well away
be nosy	geg
best	bezzy
binman	binnie
boss	gaffer
boy with on-trend hair (10–15-year-old)	ketwig
brilliant	smart
bring	fetch
broken	jarg
burgle	screw
burnt chips	scrat end

C

ENGLISH	SCOUSE
cake, Liverpool fruit	wet nelly
cash	ackers
cat	moggy
caught doing something	gripped
cause discomfort	wreck
chamber pot	jerry
chaos	choss
Christmas	Crimbo
cigarette	bifta, ciggie
cigarette, loose	loosie
clean	dig out
clever, very	dead smart
clothes	clobber
cocaine	beak
coffin-maker	boxer
cold, very	Baltic
come on	come 'ed ('come ahead')
complaint	are-eh
contraceptives	gozzie
convent	penguin house
corner shop (selling alcohol)	offie
cost	damage
cross-eyed	gozzie

D

ENGLISH	SCOUSE
dad	arl fella ('old fellow')
damage	do in
dare not	dursent
darts	arrers ('arrows')
defective	duff
detective	dick, jack (now obsolete)
devastated	devoed, devo'd
devious	sly
dialect spoken in Liverpool	Scouse
diarrhoea	runs, wild
dirty	scatty
disgusting	scatty
dodgy	sketchy
doing really well	smashing it
do nothing	sit off
doubtful quality	ropy
do you	jew
do you have any?	gorrany?
drink	sup
driver	jockey
drugs	tabs
drugs, illegal	gear
drunk	bevvied, blitzed, chemicked, kaylied, wrecked

ENGLISH	SCOUSE
drunk, helplessly	palatick
drunk, hopelessly	lushed
drunk, slightly	merry
drunk, very	rotten
dubious	shady

E

ENGLISH	SCOUSE
easy	doddle
ecstasy tablet	gary (after Gary Ablett)
electricity	lecky
empty house	emmy oggie
endearment	chuck
environmental health inspector	sanny
exactly alike	dead ringer, dead spit
excellent	boss
excellent!	sound!
excuse me!	ere!
exhausted	goosed
expression of disgust	eee

F

ENGLISH	SCOUSE
fake, also fake designer clothes	jarg
fart	boff
female pensioner	twirlie
fight	straightener
filthy	dairty
fireman	firebobby
fish-and-chip shop	chippy
five-pound note	bluey, flim
food	chuck, scoff, scran
football	footy, togga
football, an old-fashioned leather	casey
foreman	gaffer
for God's sake, shut up!	yerrokay!
found out	sussed
friend	lar
full	chokka

G

ENGLISH	SCOUSE
girl, young woman	judy (semi-obsolete)
girl, woman	doll (almost obsolete), tottie
give it to me	gizzit
give me	gimme
give us	gissa, gizza
glass of beer	jar
go on	go 'ed
goalkeeper	cat
good	laughin', sound
good health	smart
good time	crack
goodbye	in a bit, ta-ra
good-looking	fit
gooseberry	goosegog
got a	gorra
grandmother	nan (sometimes pronounced 'nin')
great	beast, beastie, smart, sound as a pound
great!	cracker!

H

ENGLISH	SCOUSE
hairdo	pairm
hands	mitts
happy	chuffed, made up
hard-faced girl or woman	Bootle buck
harm someone	bang
head	swede
headbutt	Kirkby kiss, nut
healthy	clever
he really should	eorta
heroin addict	bag'ead
hidden goods, usually stolen	stash
hide	stash
high on drugs	spaced out, stoned
home	gaff
homeless	gaffless
honest	straight (up)
hospital	ozzy
house	gaff
how are you?	ullo
hurt	wreck
husband (or male companion of any description)	feller
Huyton	two dogs fight'n

I

ENGLISH	SCOUSE
I agree	sound
I don't believe you	zarrafact?
ice lolly	lolly ice
idiot	biff, blert, bellend, get, meff, nob'ead, rem, scone'ead, soft lad
inept	cackhanded
inform, informer	grass, shop
inform on welfare cheats	sniff
injure	do in
insane	mennal
intelligence	nouse
interrupt	geg
intoxicated	messy
it will	iddle

J

ENGLISH	SCOUSE
judge	beak
just a moment!	wayo!

K

ENGLISH	SCOUSE
kick a ball badly	spoon
kid brother	kidda
know-it-all	bute

L

ENGLISH	SCOUSE
lad	lar
left-handed	cackhanded
large amount	lorra, oodles
large, intimidating person	grock
laughing a lot	in bulk
let me	lemme
light wash	catlick
little	diddy
Liverpool City Council	corpy
Liverpudlian, inhabitant of Liverpool	Scouse
loan me	lennus
loner	billy
look, to look	dekko
lots	bags

M

ENGLISH	SCOUSE
make a mistake	spoon
male wimp	big girl's blouse
Mancunian (person from Manchester)	dirty bastard
marvellous!	gear!
mate	mush, tosh, wack, wacker (now obsolete)
me	us
mean	mingy
mean person or act	arl
meatless stew	blind scouse
meat stew	scouse
Mersey ferry landing stage	lanny
mess	show
milkman	milkie
mobile phone	mobie
money	spends
mother	mam
mouth	gob
municipal rubbish dump	tip
my old friend!	miladdo!

N

ENGLISH	SCOUSE
naughty boy	buggeroo
nefarious	sly
non-Liverpudlian living in an area close to Liverpool	wool
non-Scouser	woollyback
nose	hooter
not fair!	aah-eh
nothing	nix, nutt'n

O

ENGLISH	SCOUSE
o'clock	bells
off-licence	offie
okay then	go 'ed
old	auld
older person	owl

ENGLISH	SCOUSE
old-fashioned	antwakky
our	ahr
out of	outer
out of order!	on top!
overdressed	dolled up, done up, gorrup
over-excited	tizzie
overtime	oavy

P

ENGLISH	SCOUSE
pardon?	yer wha'?
peculiar	west
penniless	brassic, skint
person, place or object which does not immediately spring to mind	doins, oojah, thingy
phlegm	grock
physical fight	it's all going off
pickpocket	dipper
pleased	made up

ENGLISH	SCOUSE
police	bizzies, filth, Z-Cars
policeman	busy, rozzer, scuffer
policemen (plural)	busies
police station	cop shop
policewoman	judy scuffer
poor person	biff
pound	nicker
pregnant	boxed, duff
present	prezzie
price	damage
price of half a pint of ale	latchlifter
prison	nick
prolonged drinking session	bender
promiscuous person	sloobag
Protestant	Prod
Protestants	Proddies
pub	ale 'ouse, boozer

R

ENGLISH	SCOUSE
really	can't half, dead, pure
really good	class
recognize	crack on

ENGLISH	SCOUSE
rent collector	rennie
residence	gaff
risky	dodgy
robber from a disreputable district	sock
rogue	scally
Roman Catholic	catlick, left-footer
rude, very	arlas
run away	bail, do one, leg it, scarper

S

ENGLISH	SCOUSE
sandwich	butty, sarney
school nurse	Nitty Nora
Scouser with a pronounced accent	lar lar
shut up!	shtum!
sibling or close relative	our kid
sir	mate
sly	skinny
small	short-arse
small change	slummie
snob	bute

ENGLISH	SCOUSE
social security	sowsh
someone prone to exaggeration	whopper
someone who doesn't come from Liverpool	whacker
someone who is physically tough	head
someone with a scruffy haircut	tatty'ead
sordid	sly
spit	gob
spoken for	took
squalid	grotty
steal	nick, rob, snitch, swipe, whip
stingy	mingy
stolen	chiefed
strike hard	lamp
student	college pud
stupid (adj.)	divvy, dozey
stupid person	divvy, space cadet, spaceman, soft ollie
sulking	cob on
sunglasses	bins
suspect goods	dodgy
suspended jail sentence	bender
suspenders	sussies
swimming costume	cozzie

T

ENGLISH	SCOUSE
take a break from work	blow
talk your way out of something or convince someone of something	blag
taxi	jobe
term of endearment for a female	queen
testicles	goolies, knackers, nuts, plums
thanks	ta
that	dat
that will	darrel
that will do	doddle
there	dur
they will	dale
thief	chief
thin legs	sparrer legs
those	dem
throw	chuck, luzz
tired	creased
toilet	khazi, lavvy, privvy
toilet, outside	petty toilet
tracksuit bottoms	trackies
trainers	trabs, trainies, webs
trousers	kecks

U

ENGLISH	SCOUSE
unauthorized time off work	bobbin
uncontrollable	tear-arse
underpants	kecks
unfair	skinny, shady
unfair, very	arlas
unfair person or act	arl
unusual	west

W

ENGLISH	SCOUSE
wait a moment!	hold on!
watch a workmate work while doing nothing	ghost
watch, surreptitiously	lamp
weakling	wet nelly
well	sound
well done!	ace!

ENGLISH	SCOUSE
well-muscled person	chest
what a	worra
what will	worral
woman (usually an old woman)	biddie
work	graft, slog
would like to	wanna

Y

ENGLISH	SCOUSE
you	yer
you (accusingly)	yew
'you know'	like
younger brother	kid brother
you (plural)	yews
you're talking too much!	mouth!

PRONUNCIATION & IDIOMS

PRONUNCIATION

The immediately recognizable features of the Scouse dialect are the congested, nasal sounds reminiscent of catarrh, together with a plaintive sing-song pronunciation where a sentence starts with a slightly whining intonation, rises questioningly in mid-sentence, ending on a higher pitch.

Additional features include:

- An adenoidal tone where 't' and 'th' become 'd', or a 'd' is added: e.g., 'id does' for 'it does' or 'dthe boss' for 'the boss.
- The ending '-y' (as in 'windy') becomes 'ee' and is pronounced with as much glee as the word itself, e.g., 'Worra classee tart!' Since 'ee' does not feature in any of the dialects which neighbour Liverpool, before the Scouse diaspora the extent of 'ee' marked the edge of the Scouse dialect area.
- Frequently mid-word vowels change sound (proper linguists call this the diphthong), adding to the lilting tone: e.g., 'Mairy likes Tony Kairtis.' ('Mary likes Tony Curtis.')
- The letters 'd' and 't' are aspirated into a lisping pronunciation with the addition of an 's': e.g., 'Dsrinkin' up time, Tsony.' ('It's drinking-up time, Tony.')

- Where lazy southerners, especially on the BBC, omit the letter 't', Scouse substitutes an alternative, usually an 'r': e.g., 'Norra nother one!' ('Not another one!)
- Sometimes 'th' becomes a 'd' or 't' to show the Irish influence: e.g., 'I wanted four, but dere's only tree.'
- As in other dialects, a 't' ending is often omitted through laziness, but Scouse changes the 't' to 'tch': e.g., 'Play tightch up frontch.' ('Play tight up front.')
- As with most dialects, the medieval Anglo-Saxon '-ing' word-end is usually dropped for the hasty 'n' instead: e.g., 'I didn't do nutt'n' ('I didn't do nothing'), with, of course, the obligatory double negative.
- The possessive 'its' becomes 's': e.g., 'The club looks after 's own.' ('The club looks after its own.')
- The letters 'l' and 'm' are often not allowed to nestle together undisturbed and so Scouse introduces a vowel: e.g., 'There's a good fillum on telly tonight.'
- At the end of a word, the letter 'k' can slur into 'ch': e.g., 'Play tight at the bach.'

- Over time, there has been a change in the Scouse diminutive with which the speaker speeds up sentences. Traditionally it meant changing the word ending to 'y' or 'ee'. More recently, the letter 'o' has been the substitute. There does not seem to be any grammatical rule to the construction of diminutive endings except that the shorter words mostly adopt 'ee' or 'y', while the longer words are shortened by 'o': e.g., Tommy Smith becomes 'Smithy', Phil Thompson becomes 'Tommo'.

- One aspect of Scouse which confuses the outside linguist is the co-existence of two different vowel sounds, best illustrated by the 'ur-air' difference. Before the great Scouse migration to other parts of Merseyside, there was a subtle nuance in the Scouse dialect between northern 'Bootle' and southern 'Toxteth' versions. The Bootle version can be heard in The Beatles' song 'I Saw Her Standing There', rendered onomatopoeically below:

And be-fore long I fell in luv with hur.
Now I'll nevur dance with anuthur,
Since I saw hur standin' thur.

- As a broad rule of thumb, the Scouse dialect becomes weaker with distance from the waterfront, although increased population movement within the city has complicated this somewhat oversimplified explanation.

- Finally, in the city's leafy suburbs and across the River Mersey on the Wirral, a softer dialect known as 'Posh Scouse' exists.

IDIOMS

The city's docks, shipyards and merchant shipping have been a rich source of idiomatic speech.

SCOUSE	ENGLISH
blowing for tugs	panting, out of breath
easy six	See golden nugget
golden nugget	Sunday overtime (much sought after extra pay not involving too much hard work)
on me hook	out of work (the docker's steel hook was an indispensable item)
sling yer hook	resign, clear off
under the lamp	paid less than the rate for the job

Two well-known Liverpool aphorisms:

1 *'Couldn't punch a hole in a wet Echo'* (a local newspaper) – a weakling

2 Passenger: *'Do you stop at the Adelphi?'* (Liverpool's most expensive hotel)
Bus conductor: *'What? On my wages?'*

The most admirable Scouse quality is the ability to quick-wittedly affix a nickname to someone, which exactly portrays that person's characteristic mannerisms, such as:

SCOUSE	ENGLISH
Diesel Fitter	the worker who keeps saying, 'Diesel fit this' or 'Diesel fit that.'
Foghorn	big mouth
Good Shepherd	checker who always sends too many sheep into his wagon
Guy Fawkes	someone who always says, 'This place needs blowing up.'
Merry Christmas	always saying 'many of 'em'
Nervous Balloon	the foreman who constantly appeals, 'Don't let me down, lads.'

SCOUSE	ENGLISH
Stanley Matthews	when lifting a packing case, a worker who always says, 'I'll take this corner.'
Surgeon	a good grafter
Tired Solicitor	always asleep on a (packing) case
Torchy	a worker who always steals batteries
Weightlifter	docker who waits while somebody else lifts the packing case
Wonderboy	someone who always says, 'I wonder what's in this case?'

PICTURE CREDITS

Alamy Stock Photo: Sabena Jane Blackbird, 3.
Shutterstock.com: danceyourlife, 4; Greens, 6–7, 87; MoreVector, 16, 79; Bodor Tivadar, 25, 59, 63; Andras Szen, 29; Mateusz Atroszko, 38; L.Rey, 54; ArtColibris, 81.